Realistic Image's In Writing.

Ideas of Photographic Realism.
By Richard Morris.

Standard Copyright License.
Copyright © Richard Morris.
First edition. Published 2011.
ISBN: 978-1-4709-3193-3

I0473770

Table of Content's

Realistic Image's In Writing.

Bibliography
1)   Edward Steichen.
2)   Yousuf karsh.
3)   Lewis Hine.
4)   Dorothea Lange.
5)   Arthur Felling, (1899-1968).
6)   Villem Flusser.
7)   Charles Sanders Pierce.
8)   Hilton Kramer.
9)   Emmanuel Kant (1724-1804).
10)   Ansell Adams.
11)   George Seurat.

Introduction.

When I first began to write about this subject I was thinking about an idea that could bring together my thoughts' on photographs' as a universal language. I thought about how people use photographs to see realism.

To make judgements' and decisions'. I started to look through photographs of photographer's whom I liked or was interested in. At the time I was interested in realism as an ideal and philosophy for viewing the world.

So I looked at a few photographers not only for their realism in the pictures they took but for the way they took picture's in general.

For instance some photographers make up there image's from ideas that are not realistic in order to question what is real.

Like Ansell Adam's overly real image's, that are over sharpened focused photograph's with the len's as a sharpening instrument.

Focused way too sharp by stopping down the lens and aperture in an effort to make the light intense thus creating the illusion of sharpness.

If the shutter is left open for very long in combination with this. Sharpness is an illusory visual effect in which we think we see so much.

That it must be real if we see a crack in the wall it must be real but instead it could be a sharpened line drawn over the wall.

This is the effect of his imagery to fool you into thinking that a landscape is real in the sense it is sharp all over.

In the foreground and background. Our eyes can only in real life differentiate one or the other at differing times not both at the same time.

Or some photographers use theatrical symbols' to show there sitter's as character's in history, and play a game of metaphor with the imagery.

In order to mean many thing's and re-enact themes' from history, or use historical figure's to play character's that are in a movie or in the publics psyche.

Which make them more popular with the wider public. Like the photographs' of Yousuf karsh. Another way might be what photographers' such as Dorothea Lange would of refused to take photographs' that would have too real an influence on the subject later on.

Because the photographs' would have been used for a promotion of a politician, getting into power by there votes and or circumstance at the time.

Whilst working for a group called the farm security administration following the plight of laid of worker's, as they slump into poverty after loosing there job's and livelihood's.

But I don't just write about photographer I write about philosophers and artist's too. Charles sander's pierce system of categorising ideas of language.

That refers' to realism which he called semiology, by using universal objects such as trees or house's as signs and symbols.

And Seurat ideas of painting with dot's to give the eye and illusion and sensation of colour, that formulate in the eye or iris as in the mind's eye.

These are all alternative routes to reality and realism almost experimental, so my idea of reality in picture's came into being.

As an idea that can reality be seen in photographs as more than a past tense, or does it create our understandings' of the real world around us like a universal language of communication.

But my main idea that is if these ideas of reality are so easy to manipulate then they are easy too misunderstand to.

So we may believe one thing when in fact it is the other. We might think that a photograph is a rigid fact but it may be a flexible articulating thing that is unrecognisable from itself and what it once was.

I use another photographers' work to show that his picture's of the poor in slums, were originally of people whom came to America chasing the American dream, only too find poverty and disillusion.

These same people may have seen image's of America or was sent them by family and friend's, what he was seeking as a photographer was the reality of these dream's.

As he was once an immigrant too whom fell into the same circumstance. So I had to ask myself what do I mean by reality, as I won't be around too see it all from begin to end and I have not been around to do so.

What I mean is a sought of truth if not an honesty with photography as an instrument, experimental or otherwise it should have some guideline's.

Or example Arthur felling look's into the face' of the rich and poor alike in the city and find's disillusionment with each other a kind of no mans land.

Is this a kind of honesty which we can't reach for with the truth. When we have created advertising we neglect to refer to our honest side to show the truth as a past tense.

Is that not how the recently unemployed worker's in Dorothea Lange's image's look at the prospect of another rich politician, promising there job's back only if they vote for him as a last hope.

But they know all politicians' lie too get there post's so why bother appealing to the truth. They seek a kind of honesty like Lewis Hine in their image's and in photography like an eye piece onto the real world.

Photography become's like realism a kind of crystal ball onto the future. But the eye play's trick's on you and so does the crystal ball onto the real world.

The truth is out of our grasp and only honesty can save our day. Ideas are all we have so what is the real. A toy we experiment with that always' get's the better of us.

The photograph is our idea of the real we use it until it gets the better of us in term's of we want to use it, some more to understand the real it misleads' us about the real world and the reality of it.

Connotatively we say we know the real, annotatively we are not certain of how to change it or use it too our best way.

In a tactile tacit sense we wish to, so that we could add and remove the real whenever we suited ourselves too or whenever it was right.

But it is more likely or just as likely to be wrong and we are possibly going to be wrong when it comes' too the question, of what is real or not to us and how too use it.

Digital photography just provokes' the problem as we all have the power to witness, and manipulate the real to our own hearts content.

We expect the photograph to follow with it's rendition of reality, any which way we want it to follow but does it precede us and reveal thing's to us that makes' us want to follow.

What is the real world, what does it have with us, read on, see what happens', seeing is believing.

Photograph's are used from day to day for different reason's so what we do with them is important, there are as much about communication as writing an idea of the real not an actual one or painting.

What did I mean by the title realistic image' in writing because photograph's are a subject in photographer's ideas, philosophy and politics'.

And help them express there ideas' about the world around them. So I wanted to write about the image's in there ideas as being real as photograph's.

Just like there is a literal idea of reality and an actual idea of reality, there is also an artist's idea of reality in painting conceptually.

I think there is a photographic idea of reality
like an ideology, Villem Flussers' idea as
image's of the reality that we walk through our
realities everyday, he believed there should be a
philosophy of photography.

Preface

On the following page outline first I talk about student life, along with my ideas. And then go onto work as ideas' on its' own, being either similar to student work.

In the sense that it is interesting or maybe exciting. Afterwards I write about photographers' and the poorer works that are displayed in galleries.

Compared to the better work that could be displayed by better photographers'. Then onto the work which I approve of as good photography and class in the term's of good photographic work or work in general.

Also I say that a photograph is fleeting in between good or bad as it is captured the outcome is undecided, left to be made into something it had not yet become or is to then become.

Afterwards I have a thought on analysis as observation in the terms' of how it can be represented by a critical view.

Then photography, painting the photographer or artist. Photographers' that are well known the type of work they do the appreciation that can be had by it.

The experimental nature of their work and other's I make personal insights in to the nature of these.

Their work, from a totally personal point of view of being photographer.
What it may mean to be a photographer or artist to myself, them and others alike.

I then write about the ideas behind imagery from text and prose, what I believe lye's within my own personal imagery.

I write about where my prose comes from and where the imagery from within my prose and text comes from, how they come about.

Also how my photographic imagery comes about in this way and surrounding my ideas and personalised view or vision of ideals.

Whilst I also look at the intricacies of other photographer's work, ideas thought, through their interpretations of the ideals around them, surrounding their imagery which remain lying within about their imagery.

Whether it be of a personal nature, an acceptable perception of photography, that reaches me from within their work.

As perspectives on the nature of photography. Prose text, writing about surrounding photography.

It is an essay surrounded by the visuality textually interpreted into photography. The idea furthermore ideals' that the photograph captures' inside of its own self imagery.

As photography, in the photographic presentation of ideology of pictures'.
Those as a conception in imagery with text.

These image's outlast the subject matter as those in which we paint our images of the world we live in projected for the way we see the world with ourselves in it.

These not being God given ideas although, they are man made ideas created as ideal's to be viewed to such an idea.

With a vision of the world around us which would imbue, other worldly notions' of ourselves within that world.

Realistic Image's In Writing.

This is about the notion that, realistic imagery in writing as photograph's outlive the sitter that the ideas' imbued in image's last longer. As the fame of actual photography itself outlast's the truer ideas', ideal's in the photographs'.

I am writing about the idea's surrounding photographic writings', the imagery brought about from within prose.

Text as is textualism of notioning, from the ideal of pictures'', writing textual notions' within writing's surrounding imagery within photography, art designed imagery writings' about imagery.

The picture writing of imagery brought forward by writing textual prose surrounding photography writing, picture writing as being a notion about textual photography.

Interpretation's of imagery understanding textually written prose about imagery, whilst myself writing my studies in photography, art, designed still photography, life opinion's as a photographer.

I decided to write about the imagery, prose, that text brings' about of which is surrounded by imagery from within textuality itself, textually.

From the sitters' point of view the photograph alone becomes' more famous for its technical outreach, standards' of ability or probability.

For instance a famous sitter in a portrait would be outlived by the photograph taken of himself. The very fact the imagery had been difficult to capture or had been taken by a famous photographer.

Whom had made several varying technical standards' or leaps with his camera's technology. By of course pushing the camera to a variety of achievements'.

Maybe the advent of colour or an ideal, such as the distribution of manageable information circumferencing the advent and increase of poverty.

In a particular area or period of time, this is an ideal of the mass distribution of information and detail in a particular locality.

Some photographer's also use the esteem of their sitters' to make themselves more famously esteemed as photographers'.

The photograph they then make of the sitter in future, in turn creates a more famous air of esteem for the photographer.

Whom becomes more enwrapped in the sitter's esteem and fame himself. Which then would make the photographer, his photographs more famous than the sitter or future sitters' himself.

The fact the photographers' photograph is of a famous person with equaling esteem mean's that the photograph holds more value.

As a quality piece of photographic imagery because the photographer can claim to have imbued the photograph, with its' qualities, esteemed value of high regard held in favourable opinion.

Also there is the fact that he had photographed several famed esteemed people as sitter so that imbues', the imagery as a collection of sociable interaction between famous people as his sitters', photographer alike.

A writer and photographer's life stands' between that of a workers life. A life which start's or ends', at the beginning and end of the day until night.

It as a life is neither one that is similar to a normal working day or one which is like a normal nights rest.

As a stills' photographer I do not take a part in the normal working day to night schedule. The moments' of forgetting what went before me, a passivity of a photographic still moment.

Fleeting disappearance of a time routine I have no wish to collect other ideas or ideal's as those of my own.

I wish to create ideas as a personal nature of self, not necessarily of my own individuality. As a writer and photographer, I was not apart of the normal social working routine, as other worker's are.

Whom work in routine structures around daily, nightly schedules. Have neither worries, or care's about that routine which is as important to them as the work.

Which lye's within that routine scheduling in which they are within, though that life in which a writer and photographer works' in.

Researches', has to in some way come together. Not simply as a routine but as a whole, not separately an unnecessary part of a whole.

This rationality of reason in the routine act's for the whole yet as a writer and photographer I realise.

I do not share in the celebratory moment, of the work which go's on about me. Into the loss of forgettable presentary moments'.

Neither do I take a part in the whole ideals of work. The present day understandings of living, life working as a schedule.

Also an ideology of life, with life living from an ideal of forgetting the presentary moment's of these ideas as a whole theme.

The whole being the idea of work itself an expression, the value being as presented to the self, In order to understand the world.

The self has then to be expressed too, most workers' like alcoholics' working in order of forgetting what then had past before them.

I as a writer and photographer worked in a contradiction to forgetting in order to remember what notion of myself, has past before me.

What remains' behind me a problem or difficulty to find, what may present itself in front of me. The normal person's working life which is unchecked usually, willfully goes unnoticed by the average worker.

Although as a writer and photographer I imply, I am a worker of an inventive manner, what I want to produce and present is always new.

I am usually in a celebration of these ideas, ideal's, in terms of reordering them for a greater understanding with a belief in them.

I place in them my ideas by the use of prose as I become more understanding of these and many other ideas or ideals', I begun to realise how they become more ordered.

This of course is to me not a greater understanding of this order, but though still the greater celebratory structure of the ideas as prose.

As ideas in prose not merely pieces of a schedule, although I also think is the sort of thing that may be, what would be missing from the working day or night of me as the worker.

Realistic Image's in Writing. By Richard Morris.

I do not only create an understanding from things' that had place and purpose for anyone other than myself. In fact mostly what I do can be noticeably viewed by what surrounded me for age's.

They are from peopled place's which I believe have mattered to me. I in that way am proud of these peopled, places' in order to inspire my feelings' of them in my work.

I continue researching ideas for my prose about photographic imagery. Are not only reminder's to the present moment but from also day, night the past and present.

They had the same importants' remain in order of this, celebrations of ideas and ideals'. To see from within this rationality, reason not something already in usage.

Then already having had being lost forgotten about, in disregard because of it's' age whether old or new.

Although too present to myself a usage in the present momentary ideas, ideal of the nature or work itself, so I as a photographer of work with still imagery and textuality.

Write prose about text in order to see the momentary still imagery which lye within the work of prose, stilled photograph.

My photographic Imagery is about the momentary imagination that prose produce I do this as a way of inventing, yet although what I am inventing is as personal.

From a moment which may be from stilled imagery textual, imaginary the past or present, although as still imagery.

Textual imaginary moments' of prose withdrawn from a structural part of my own photography.

An idea of the momentary still image moments' occur I try not to put these ideas of time in a place, in order to then loose them.

Disregardingly as having belonged to any other. I would only see my personal ideas as being of some use to me.

Not anyone other than myself, I believe that these thoughts', feelings' in themselves had with my own reasoning.

Throughout my own day and night life within myself, itself remains' with several presentary thoughts' feelings' moments' of still images imagined textual.

This as it may seem is the way I may see myself reliving my work, moments' of still imagery photographically, textually of my own personal thought on a photographic still image.

A personalised self invention throughout imaginary notion's of an idea is a realisation, of what is then produced presented.

What I present or invent is often recognisable by it being itself of a personalised nature, the momentary still photograph is viewed envisioned.

Not only from what I write and read remains' the same when photographed as still imagery, of a similar moment then is also still photography.

Which may be viewed only by what I perceived to have had previously viewed, envisioned as a photograph then had later captured on film.

It is the imaginary moment of the still photograph that lye's within what has beforehand been textaulised into a idea of by my own prose.

To me is a still photographic image of textuality as prose textualised still imagery, textual still imagery photographic work to me fundamentally writing about photographs'.

Not only of importance to me but really as it is a simplifiable nature, merely by a recognition of its' own importance of simplicity.

The nature as such an expression is only a way of simplicity of the work, the work how it is done, also had greater importance than work in itself.

I produce and present my work photographically, by a photographic still image. Wishing to create a reality of the still image outside of what would lye within itself as photographic realistically still image in the use of prose.

A lot of my imagery is taken from several moment's of my own personal writing, photographic life by living as a writer photographer, is from the writing of my photography.

The photographic imagery of a still picture I create is mainly realistic, in the sense that I try not to manipulate its gift for inventing a kind of realism.

A straight photographic still imagery that presents some of the stilled moments not passively produced unfleetingly.

I wish also to inventively create through the textuality of prose, on my photographic work a realistical moment which will remain within itself.

As to present or produce a personal sense of itself as a piece of work for myself, I use my work for a personal celebrational moment's envisioned throughout the day and night time.

Although I have my own explanation and opinion's of photographical still imagery I present in my work.

I continually produce photographic still image as a visualised textuality, photographing still imagery through the usage by my prose.

Textually such as which I have written prose about realistically of textual imagery, being a textuality as still photography.

It has been my way of being a photographer and writer I have throughout, this way of my writing ignored this sense of image and textuality.

In the normal day and life of a working man, at work in his own particular working placed environment.

Worked in a complex way simplified by in reality being a photographer and writer, whom can easily create a professionalised understanding.

Through his writing and photographic still imagery, to in a sense recreate my writing as a photographic textuality of my own imagery.

Though I have photographed whilst writing, about my own photography only needing to do so is both textual and photographical.

Alhough writing about a personal textuality this way avoids' the momentary view of being a photographer writing, about a writer's and photographers' life their way of living as in textual still photographic imagery.

Possessing the momentary ideas which I hold, itself as being from within thoughts' of most importantly a photographer, writer my ownself textualising still imagery.

So in these term's I am writing about my views'
on photographic textuality, view's of
photographic still imageries textuality prose,
writing itself.

This is the way I write about photographic still
picture's, textuality in a sense of a
photographers' textualisation in his writing.

Writing from what I photograph as still
pictures', what I write as the part of a whole as
the whole personal realistic, textuality viewed
with momentarily way of how I photograph a
still not of work as a whole ideal.

I thought I would write about real life
experience's that I have lived through provoked
thought, about which has lead too my thinking
about circumstance's.

I could not had predict there happening's in an
effort to then predict there outcomes', but too
make useful attempt's to observe them as
circumstance then peculiarities.

Too then continue the process of my photographic projects', which they as a circumstance may have threatened.

The idea is not to be prevented from the act of achieving my aim's, too follow them keeping all remnants' of that aim in tact.

Obviously the circumstance is mine to view through these ideas in order too then both gain by learning something, of the unusual naturalness of viewing these circumstance's may have on me.

In this way I must not assume that the idea has become new to me, as viewed too my mind but, to also presume it has substance had previously been viewed.

Textually as an imaginary still photograph, that this as a circumstance has only reached my minds view for that moment.

Too me in this way I can then see thing's in appearances' around me as they are, unprovoked in their natural states', or truer naturalness a state of mind.

Although this is not a practice I would also use without a method of applying to, a mass of knowledge.

For instance by the use of a camera I can create an amount of collective detail, information on film, in view of the camera.

I would then alter this film in a way either too recreate the circumstance I was then to see. As through a circumstance of that which the camera had viewed though further the truth.

Or reasoning behind the event as a photographic image. This rationalising of such a circumstance could have also lead me to change in other ways, to reveal details interpret the information.

In another way in the reuseage of knowledge that had to become mine. This would then hopefully lead me to a mass, collective.

Information from my camera by the use of technical capabilities' of the photographic materials that I can find possible to have had some reusage as in roll film.

This it seems would be the textual abilities from within a photographic still whilst placed in the camera.

I then believe in the importance in seeing myself as a part of the day, afternoon and night in observing my alienation.

Indivisibly from other socially, commonable are as of lives which go on around me this, alienisation.

The camera would join these other ideas, personal ideals together. Separating the ideas of alteration or change in this sense into being.

So they stay the same without so called invention as a discovery. My own personal photographic stills' does not in reality fit into any definitive contextuallised ideals'.

Although it is through, by ideas and ideals which they can be seen in a construction of themselves as an imagery of my own creativity. In appearance to the viewer those whom view it as merely a fleeting structure.

This I think is an important of my own still photography, because it allows me to continue within it.

Is not held up by the ideas in which it holds as the possessor, possessive nature of a photographic ideal.

I can alteringly change in case, of any misshappenings' in day to day life and of course living.

I would add to any impressed on colour, colouring tonality texture or gleam from the natural chemistry of elements surrounded by the still photography, I wish to enrapture.

Such a theme as the weather in a still photograph would lead me into a theme. Of the success that the representation would have in, also the possibility of the realisation of that theme as imagery.

Atmospherics within a photographic still is usually a part of the imagery. That I have to alter in a way too present any eventual outcome as a further interpretation.

Off the photographic stills' imagery whether it maybe ideological, theoretical or of a technical demonstrative nature.

The stills' photograph has to pick it up within the film then later gain some realistic presentation.

By the photographers' controls of the process. Beginning with if what I have capture could be viewed as being realistical.

To in a sense interpret to myself what is real, what is not realistic in the still imagery I am attempting to present.

This would then eventually make justifications on what I allow myself to produce, Some imagery is not worth its eventual outcome.

Only due to the atmospherics in the photographic stills' imagery such as tonality, shadow and shade.

These colours that it would eventually produce or then saturation and contrast of gradation the imagery as a picture may not be fully realised.

As I would view it as a stills' photographer, a picture of an atmospheric still image such as ice cold elements, or sunlight gleaming through the window.

These as a picture would create the likely problem with contrast of the intensity as the light reflected in the images every shades.

The amount tonality in the imageries tonal range, colour density in quality as it's' saturation.

I do not usually know if this is an easy picture to create. Though I would need to more than generally, think about making a picture out of these as elements.

To me still imagery is more than what it appears to be. Usually ends up as what I would have attempted too prevent myself from imagining.

Because the strengthening of imagery clarification of the clarity in the imagery. So in this way I can usually complete an image knowing that the imagery has carried itself .

I had carried myself that much further, this in itself is a justifiable reason for making Photographic still imagery.

Presenting it and producing a finer still image of photographical textuality of prose on my photography as a photographer writing as a writer about photography writing.

I would take a still picture with thought to change it in some way so that I could continually think about it in a mechanical, methodical form through my prose.

In a view to alter it by using the idea as apart of the photographs' visual textuality. Trying to follow the elements' surrounding, within the imagery depending on what has made me take the image in the first place.

I would then decide on what would demonstrate a change or alteration within it. Light intensity, image clarity by chemical engineering at the processing development stage.

The use of several differing in quality lens can create even producing a better presentation to produce such a still of imagery.

I do have to use my knowledge of what I have learnt before hand not rely on the so called gift of fates'.

Still photography is a very old medium when I view imagery from the several different varying periods produced as captured by photographic imagery.

As stills' photography it in itself is an almost supernatural experience. This sought of approach to the viewing off photographic still, imagery.

Is quite unusual mainly because the idea of trying to exercise my imagination by ideas of choice is the same as being within the creative process.

Of piecing together a personal idea a personal ideal of how the world around me should appear to be, really how the world is as it is also apparent to me.

So as an example, of how I would believe the world to seem too also appear to me, arranged in a selection of imagery chosen by me.

Doing so choose by selection of the still images from past, present and future still picture's.

I could in fact be creating an idea of the world that is uniquely of my own choosing or rearranging.

That would be very much different considering the particular choices I decided continued so on to make.

To a variety of ideals' I may present to myself, of myself. This kind of exercise's, are a common approach for me too undertake.

When viewing mine or someone else' still imagery, I would first begin by looking at the world of a stills' imaginary of visually graphic presentation.

Then want to decide on that choice, what way these images came about not only visually but also technically.

Some of the old techniques used in photographic stills' I would consider worth using, attempting today.

Not only to see if they were possible to work with but to find out if their standards were possible to achieve, with the same comparison's in quality of more modern techniques.

Standards

Only because the standards demanded by the individual photographer's I am attempting to follow in this way by writing about. Were extremely high in quality which I as a photographer visiting photographic stills' exhibition.

Viewing modern day photographer's have not seen anything as similar in standards. The still imagery is such a comparison of, technical quality that it is nowhere near a match in fact it is so far of, that it is more than a mere wonder.

At why in these photographic stills, exhibition the images are called photographic. Mainly because they seem like comparatively faint sketches of reality.

Where as the past photographic stills' imagery is so complete an image that there is no need for extra comment.

But an extra time in which to contemplate there splendour and wonderment at here completeness of reproduction off realities a realisation of the imagination.

I could probably attempt to place these photographers' of differing qualities from differing periods. I would become even more greatly confused at the comparison in standards'.

Because of being given to be believed that photography has technically travelled forward in technological standard's since the time of these stills' photography.

The photographer's photography I am writing about in an appreciating mood, are the ones' that modern day photographer had not taken.

The photographers' still photography I write about mentioning in this mood. Had taken far greater technological advantage of their times, than any other of the photographers'.

I could write in today's photographic market place, personal photographic exercises in technique in private.

It seems as though the standards I write about are in accordance with excesses in technique when compared to modern day photographic stills' exhibition. Individual works of photography.

Seem to have been given more work on than some photographers' whole lifetime work. In today's modern use of photography the standards of quality and acceptability dropped into a disappearance, are of a sinking spiral.

I also believe that it is the demand from the market place that has done this not the opposite. Which is to increase the standards of quality not to produce an example of how that can be further produced.

Like other things surrounding me now such as ideas, ideals which ask for a decrease in their excess.

Not an increase in excessability this view only presently produces a practicably useless example of following, the particular practice in which I find the comparisons.

Myself

I believe as a photographer would prefer to view a valuable vision of photography when I wish to view photographic imagery in an art, photographic gallery exhibition.

For instance by comparing the modern standard of photography in galleries of today by photographers' of the past too today's photographer's of the present day. The standard and quality are of in this way different measures.

There work challenge's what it mean's to be photographing reality, and what it mean's to be seeing reality, how realty is interpreted.

I sit all in the mind, externally internally what does reality really mean in picture's. Photographically is it similar to art.

Can it simply be viewed through a len's as reality, painted in art. Does it have to be questioned first like an interrogation, left too be believed.

Edward Steichen

In the past a photographer, artist such as one like Edward Steichen, whom had started his photographic practice as a freelance photographer in the US United States of America's navy.

Edward Steichen created the conceptual ideal of World War 2 photography as the heroics' of a no win deal a dead loss circumstance. Of the war photography, image's he found around in World War 2.

He brought this to the Hollywood studios with dramatic lighting for heroes or heroines' alike. Which still exists' today is followed as such along the exact same line's too finite detail.

In Hollywood stylised make up, also lighting created by him when he himself had been the portrait photographer for the studios of Hollywood.

What is called a permanent presentation of the heroic image. This is also an image of a world view to imagery as seen through the eyes of one single individual.

Then later on whilst in work for a big Hollywood portrait studio or advertising agencies company, turning out thousands' of imagery as portraiture on varying occasions'.

Which does not happen in todays' present day, most photographer's which later exhibit in galleries start the practice of portraiture.

In or from small self funded studios not in a big industrial outlet such as those provided by Hollywood studios.

Yousuf karsh

Even the great portraiture photographer, Yousuf Karsh whom emigrated from Turkish Armenia in 1925 to Canada. Had been operating his own portraiture studio, for ten years in Ottawa, attempted to create a worldly vision.

Through his access to the leading most international figures in the then theatre of War, on into other selected circles had set an example which endured for a further six decades.

His signature approach to formal portraiture with dramatic lighting established from his study, of great paintings in Boston collections.

Came also from experiments' in stage lighting after being a photographer, for theatrical productions for the Ottawa drama league in the 1930s.

Yousuf Karsh photographed portrait subjects of power in which the individual could not fail to overcome, overpower a dead loss circumstance.

Through government leadership by distribution of that said same self notion of power in the individual, whom he photographed as such worldly sitters' in a portrait with such a view envisioned over that world.

Used the fame and esteem of the great subjects of his portraiture like the Hollywood stars actors or writers such as H.G.Wells, 1943.

Actresses, starlets alike Beatrice Lillie (Lady Peel), 1948. Internationally renowned famous names in government as prime ministers' such as Winston Churchill 1941.

To in this sense becomes' a famous photographer himself. Although having said this his work as a photographer is technically proficient to the subject.

Though I have seen and prefer better mastering of the technical capabilities of the photographic material he uses.

I would have had preferred him to have gained his fame from this ability alone rather than the ability to gain an appointment for the portraiture of a famous person.

Although this is more often true of today's photographer whom started from minor position as of course so did many a photographer start of at first with a very minor freelance position.

As a prime example of an individual gallery photographer, having had a uniquely high standard of work which has not been compromised.

Whilst photographer's which exhibit in Galleries today don't rise to, surpass. Or make any comparison at the standard produced.

The likes of such photographer's as with a more individual personal approach to their photographic work whilst still attempting to compete by leading the competition.

In a more commercialised view to personal photographic artistic work at least this type of work.

As a way of working is not seemingly considered, to be the more successful way of making an approach to commercial work.

Artists' and photographers' whom work like this are more likely to be considered as having achieved some success creatively, in this way a critical commercial sense of the term.

As having some sense of leading a creativity, in the commercialised term's of artistic, photographic creativity.

This could also be considered as an imagery of creativity, as I have not mentioned a writers' sense of the term creativity.

Being admired as having some individual artistic merit so in this sense for me the one idea, which has come from these comparisons'. Is that even though I may have to compete with such a standard of work in portraiture.

That has been supported by a big photographic industrial outlet, such as in the past the Hollywood studios film industries. The advertising agency as a company.

I can still attempt to produce my own personal work to a gallery standard such as the photographers' of past, because I believe in this sense.

Of a personalised view or vision of creativity and imagery, that the individuals desire to do things for himself is ultimately, capable of producing a higher standard of quality in their work.

As a self funded gallery photographer than a photographer whom is apart of a commercially funded larger industrial studio.

Which I write to make these such averaging claims on, photographic stills' directing. As an idea written in text, a photographical kind of writing.

The textual writing on photography I am thinking about is observing an idea, idealogy or a concept.

Such as work hour's, making still imagery of these for those times when I do not grasp an understanding of what is happening textual.

In the observational contextuallity of the working hours' as these maybe either day or night hours which I have not previously viewed.

Envisioned working hours throughout an imaginary ideal. The still imagery is brought about in order to create a further vision of my textualisations'.

I use the technical film processes to enhance a view that is a focus onto quality of idea that has taken place.

Whether it be an expression of a face or architecture in the cityscape landscape or seascape.

A main important view is the technique in which I produce this vision then use it as embodied within my text.

Realism is photographical; it displays a still image of phenomena which is obvious when it is around me and my view.

For instance in advertising still imagery, these advertising images offer there phenomena as a product to the clientele.

The phenomena come from within the imagery as a view to a vision, created by the realism of still photography.

Whether it be love of the opposite sex, sensuality of a product such as perfume. The ideal of another life, freedom of a new landscape, city shores,' leading to differing Ocean.

Although all this seems' freeing and unembodied. Still photography does have some of its own ideals and ideologies, for example what it deals with alone.

Separately form ideas of still imagery a visionary
Symbolic depiction, such as text and painting
The realism alone is stunning when produced
within the right quality of reproductive
contextualised presentation.

This presentational whether it be from the
disciplines of technical reproduction standards of
processing and printing.

Also in textual forms of writing and meaning
implied upon an image such as the ideals of
religion or religiously inclined thinking and
thought.

Through text from the religious media or the
media of a similar nature still photography as it
stands is used in our society to offer the
phenomena it places on display.

As an ideal to the form within that of which he or she has viewed it a perfect view or formation of the vision viewed as it is on display.

Therefore on offer to the viewer to hold in his personal vision, as would be to have seen or placed in awe of as something in which the viewer can then own.

The phenomena which is in this way displayed as a photograph is that of an object which can then be reproduced in several varying forms'.

For example I would not be just simply reproducing a stills' photograph as a plain paper but as an indication of such ideals.

As of mind notional time or space with formation of shapes and lines. Perception as in the ideas which lead the imagination.

The illusions with the notions as fantasy in sexuality through beauty to ugliness seen as being good and evil. Within imagery of the imagination, also lead me to an understanding of these ideals.

Form a particular perspective or argument given by me as a stills' photographer from within a visual context.

Photography of stills' from within the visual text's, context of interpreting what is inside of a language as a argument in which realism off stills' photography may find challenging in place of advertising.

I mean that in this sense a stills' photographic realism can interpret what is the fundamental meaning that can be found from in the textual context of a language.

Visualised through a prose about text from within a textuality or visualisation surrounding that language.

A photographer at work in the studio or on a landscape type of setting is usually singularly working on an idea or from his point of view.

I as a photographer of stills' would attempt to separate other interfering ideas from my point of view and concentrate on my personal visionary ideal.

In order to express my level of concentration upon personal vision. About the working environment I had created and placed myself within surrounding me. I would believe most of my favourite stills' photographer's or photographic artists'.

Would have done the same which is what firstly more than the work I actually do or achieve, makes me most comfortable.

Is that the fact that other photographers' do the same in order to achieve their own personal working standards'.

Is to observe other stills' photographers' at work, but only on their own do they do this so as not to disturb the work that is being approached.

So although I try to work alone separate from other people at work I do acknowledge the standards' of levels' of work.

In the sense I would attain a level of that standard off work from myself that my own observations' seem acceptable to me.

Although the feeling of separation from other workers' whom are photographers' or maybe not photographer's in the working environment.

Does lead me to have thoughts' of contradictory ideals'. I do attempt to achieve all the variable standards' of quality and achievement.

That does bring my work to similar intricacies of which involve differing, methodological treatment of ideals such as time spent on the work I do.

As in the amount of hours I spend on a particular work, for instance a picture that could affect my dissatisfaction can open up other virtualities in technique.

From the processing stages back through to the beginning of picture taking process itself needing maybe a truer filtration.

To the viewing points I feel is missing within the final personalised visionary imagery. Through which I am trying to pick from in the proposed picturing further renditioning values from.

In the viewing of the final imaginary vision of that photographic stills' picture, I think that there are ideas as thoughts and feelings.

That I would like to communicate which are fleeting, although the concept of these ideas would be around for a lifetime.

And the way to express communication of these concepts' are from within the ideal of works'. As an imaginary vision rather than the simplicity of thought and feelings as a view to an idea there is the complexity.

Of a continuingly lasting concept of expressing or impressing the need, want or will to communicate the fleeting smaller ideal.

To the lastingly larger conception of a vision, I am going to write about the thoughts or thinking which makes my day to day ideas, of work more humour in and from a more awe inspiring view of a contextualised view of work.

In the approach that can also bring these ideas within a context to create the fascination of the working environment. From the points of view of my own experiences'.

These moments of still photography are of severally, produced in kind to draw together into a fascination.

For the beliefs in the enjoyment that I get contextually, of reverie that can bring about also the awe inspired fascinations in it, repetitively can be creative.

And as an ideology of these ideas the humour I can find in enjoying in an ideal as it is lying, in contextual visions' of the working environments'.

Which inspire awe for humour fascination for the enjoyment of the comparison of ideas into working. Although in this comparison is the contextual idea of many ideologies of working environments'.

Though only from a view point of my own contextually a fascination with humour, awe and enjoyment as the main contextual theme.

It is an adult humour that is not about what the photographer is trying to photograph but that he is photographing something he knows.

But that the fact that he can photograph something which will later come out showing to be as capturing something later which can then be discussed.

The humour is that he doesn't know what he is photographing until it had been photographed. Lived the longevity of its life as many things as that something in itself which it had been photographed for.

It is as if the photographer creates' a life for that thing which he can not predict the outcome of that life form for that thing in itself. I like to work not to conclude ideas that are not yet whole.

For instance the best still photography is usually by the photographer's. Which capture pictures at moments in time when the images describe neither one or the other description.

Of the subjects' depicted in time it is a sought off shallow grey ground which the image revealed is descriptive to the true nature of the events depicted.

Stills' photographer's like images, Show people neither living for the day yet captured for posterity.

Lewis Hines &, Dorothea Lange

Like the photographer's of the documentary photography writing from photography the imagery of Lewis Hines personally produced photographic imagery.

Dorothea Lange production of work about imagery writing from, for the government agency the farm security administration.

The imagery of these two photographer's Lewis Hine, Dorothea Lange. Remains symbolic of the circumstances in poverty beyond the point of view bestowed, by the actual sitters presented in the imagery through poverty.

They also stand as symbolism for future picture's of poverty from the images by the poor. As an image in pictures they will in this way outlast the sitters in the photographs by these photographer's.

To be used to render other images of the poor in poverty portrayed as sitters, in similar imagery. By similar photographers' in kind to Lewis Hine, Dorothea Langes' portrayal as to what may be rendered in the terms of subject matter.

In this same sense these images are of observational rendering's of documentations portraying previously sought after subject matter.

They as images bestow an idea of outliving a circumstance which for these people as unable themselves to survive the moment itself. The still images taken of them threaten to outlive those the images were taken from.

Or of to survive as images in themselves the then same sought circumstantially, the stills' photographer's take these images.

To show the ideologised realism the stills' photograph of the photographer could take from circumstances which were before him.

Still' images outlasting to the present day the meaning that would lye inherent in them, the very ideology which it was supposed to stand for.

The imagery it had been taken from, the people which had by mishap created these idealisation's of being poor attempting to survive.

Are in this particular circumstance unable to keep their own particular ideal as protectively assured for posterity as an image that the camera evokes of them in themselve's.

To remain as unspoilt as the images that these people must have went through several horrors throughout their life time before and after these images.

Yet these are untold unpresented they are certainly not as respected or admired, as there are images of photography in themselves.

Anyone looking at these images would ordinarily not give the person in them a second glance or second moment's thought.

Although the images of them must have been looked at on several occasions by the same person.

The people in them or others' alike them would not have given themselves any more of a glance to themselves than they would have given any of other the persons in them.

So what is it about photography that make a person viewing, them look a second time or makes a great photographer neither want or wish.

To explain whether the images are of a finite idea circumstance or of an infinite ideal of a circumstance.

A circumstance he look's for that will not tell the photographer himself whether the imagery are of one or other circumstance.

Which it often is attempting to neither capture and portray as one rather than the other circumstance.

Though only to try and truly settle somewhere, between this shallow grey grounded area. Because as an image it portrays' a true or truer feeling, of the circumstance by doing so in this way.

The still photograph then captures a moment of the photographer's by the cameras own making.

I feel that this is in this way a great photographic presentation of what may then lye in an image of a still photographic picture.

It show's the circumstance undecidedly deciding for itself the outcome of the image not the photographer creating an answer for the photographer himself. As an excuse for what is then about to happen within the imagery.

I do not like images created to explain what lye's within them by the photographer and do not in this way think that they are of great still photography.

Like my own images of students that show images of people at either one or other stage of their working life.

With neither the ability to be successful or as
failures unsuccessful, but as students they are
people whom lye between a shallow ground and
grey area as to what the outcome of their studies
might be.

Their working life routine has not been revealed
to them as either a success or failure though
somewhere in between, there lye's a cycle of
productivity.

Which for me is difficult enough to reveal
though capable of being photographed by me.
Although they lack some of the esteem of a
professionals working persons life and character
they still for me show the same unpredictability.

Which lye's apparent in few of the moments that
appear in a persons working life. Of uncertainty
at the outcome which is sooner or later revealed
by that predetermination off his actions.

Yet this is still, though there may be of a few moments the type of photograph I would wish to capture and portray.

An unfiltered, unwatered down version of realities real life eventualities in a persons living life.

Like the people in stills' photography, my images of still photography of students life at university is likely to outlive any of the views which may have been held by the students themselves or of me as a student.

Although the ideology of being a student at university with a particular point of view or vision will outlive those students and I as a student in these images and photographs as an ideal.

These photographs I have taken may survive anything the students, I may go through and what they had been taken of longer.

More securely safer than anything the students, I as a student might had attempting to survive through as an ideal in themselves.

When I decide to take a photographic still I make varying attempts to assume the change they may make on me and my personal experiences'.

Like when I write about my photographs or other peoples' photography I persuade myself along the way through the sentences or paragraphs' within the prose I am writing.

That there are changes I am making or about to make with the examples I demonstrate therein from within my writing technique.

This I believe should hold the same as true from within my photographs and my views' with other photographic imagery.

Arthur Felling

Weegee was his nickname, had been born in Poland as Arthur Felling living from 1899-1968. I could say that Weegee shows a realism of view in the world through imagery.

Differing from that of Hollywood & media images. His technique is a more about realistic immediatecy than of any other technical detail of the camera, more an optically produced realism than a mechanical production of reality.

A presentation of imagery without particular or peculiar heroes with heroines, but where everyone seems too had been a loser of loss without any gain.

A vision of the world that has nothing to gain in a synthetic realisation of people with more to work towards than to work away from.

In terms of points of view as a vision of reality, although as a realisation it is merely a view not an accomplishment worthwhile in a social or community wise; of the sense.

More of societies communities breaking apart at the seam's rather than coming together, as we are brought up to believe in.

Media viewed visioning of termed sense, meaning by world through imagery as this term the world, so it is hard to be an individual with terms of being in a media social community.

When a vision once viewed had been taken as sensed permanence is given such moments of temporality, that envisions' an encompassing notion.

Involving loosing that which has previously been seen to be gained, as a media vision viewed socially communal.

The world viewed visioning an individual's uncalmitus right of a through way, to self independency by democracy seeing a realisation through the fictitious.

So this way it is hard to make a view visioned through the mass media, but there can be a personal view envisioned throughout the mass media.

Villem Flusser.

A German professor of media communications named Villem Flusser though believes that writing and text hold imagery within themselves or from within themselves as a whole body of text or works'.

Which in themselves can be manipulated either way to hold a series of truth's or lies' which can be seen to be there main beliefs. That hold for me the same elements of persuasion.

So to me the idea or sense of manipulation can sway either way between an ideal and explanation of momentary acts of meaning throughout an ideal.

In this sense of an ideal or idea of a manipulation in circumstances', from within a photograph and text ideal of imagery.

I attempt to change within a momentary circumstance to reveal the sense that which I have found a manipulative example of these or both of the same ideas imagined by Villem Flusser.

Which I believe maybe present though it had offered itself as its' manipulative sense, of either truthfully or falsely having a hold on the circumstance.

Or the manipulative nature of sense which the circumstance presents' to itself, as a moment of still imagery in my work.

In this sense presents itself to me as either through its use of varying ideas from the manipulative natures of photography and text. As moment's from within the imagery of both, truthfully or falsely manipulative.

Created circumstances' as though they were these momentary still images from therein the photography, text that have a hold on the ideal of these from within themselves.

The main ideals which make up these ideas are of photography and text. I try with the use of these ideas to alter the use of manipulation or sense, of these momentary stills', imageries.

In an effort to view the circumstance's of these ideals which may be seen from within them, to remain a photographic and of textual moments as imagery.

Although undecipherable without the manipulative use of these ideals myself as the photographer, or writer of text on these circumstances'. From a personal description which may be then seen to be beliefs'.

For instance the boundaries between normal modern day realities, ideals' taken for granted nowadays'.

Are now found whilst approaching a very thin drawn line between realities' misconception's. From the visual point of view there is the artist merit of values of photography throughout realism.

Many photographs represent the realistic values, ideals of our modern view or vision of the world. Although these image's of the real within photography are interpreted by ourselves, as a product of the seemingly everyday view.

A vision in those such images are of the real world as viewed through these other such like imagery.

When I see an image of a landscape taken by photography I then believe it to be real. Though I know from my experiences' in an artistic, photographic background.

That there is just so much room for doubting the very same imagery as being there is for having the said same belief in those images, as imagery of art and photography.

Obviously imagery can now with modernised technological presentational mimickery, such as computer imagery and chemically based substances.

As in the processes of photography produced parts' and product's of an image to create certain visually based, belief systems'.

Of visionary aspectation and or expectations' within us so as to make appear a reality. A make up or mish mash of ideas that would appear like a jigsaw puzzle.

Differing parts of an image can be taken apart, then   assemble to create a seemingly original landscape or other image.

In which one would conjure up ideas of it belonging to a real live subject from within the modern day conceptions' and ideologies' of realities in the world.

Charles Sanders Pierce.

The American philosopher Charles Sander's Pierce (1839-1914) is quoted as saying that proposition is true if it is reality which is the efficient cause of our sensation.

Pierce is remembered for his teleogical account of truth, for founding pragmatism, for contributing to formal logic and for pioneering work in the theory of signs (semiotics).

Pierce had been a practicing experimental scientist impressed by the way scientific concept is mainly precise by being tied to observable consequences of observations'.

It had also been along these lines that he formulated (1878) the general maxim for achieving clear ideas identifying it as the core pragmatism.

Both his pragmatism and his work were embedded in a theory of signs on the idea that the meaning of a sign is its power. Too determine observers' of it; to interpret it in also a determinate fashion.

Ansell Adams

By looking at the imagery of a photographer such as Ansell Adams photography of landscapes I can see that the lens' he uses' in which to produce his imagery are for the purpose of differential focusing.

And the aperture he chooses on these len's are designed and then installed to give a finite idea of what sharpness can clarifyingly achieve within his imagery.

These overly real and sharp images illustrate a landscape to us which can be too close to the truth to be of the real.

They are altogether too sharp and crisp for the human eye to perceive at one go from within the foreground and from there within the background.

The ideal he reproduces in these imagery of sharpness can only be captured as a presented image. Or imagery of the real world and of also the real as an ideal which we can then perceive as done this way.

So this is a way for landscape photographer's, may like to question other artists' illustrator's or literary figures'.

Whom use imagery, within their work to the value and true nature in their individual perceptions of the real world, which these imageries are perceived.

In one sense this in itself devalues the products of photography for the value which lays' within it and, it in itself no longer seems to confront that which we believe or hope to believe to be real, of the real world.

Though it does also as well allow us to not make pretence at what our minds also perceive to be real. And can in this way ask us many more questions, of ourselves.

And are previously so, taken for granted perceptions of ourselves and the world around us given for or to the real.

Also photographers' such as those which create celebrity images that are of also notionalised lives and part of media imagery are not the type of pictures'.

I am writing about textually as is of being of imagery and the imaginary hopes of a life such as in the imagery of photographer writers and artists'.

George Seurat

And also imaginary, Imagery hopes of an artist, painting as such is divisionism. Of George Seurat 1859-1891, and his dots and contrasting colours'; oils' on canvas revolutionary technique from an observational point of view which does not include analytical observation.

Although preferring one; observation, and not the other analyses. I try to interpret my photography, text as imagery mentioning in the textual form as being about other worldliness ideas of work and photography as an essay on uplifting and downy nature of work.

As being of the adult humour or amusement, put in some images of work in which correspond with the ideas or ideals of images of work.

So as to be in line with views such as photographers' such as Dorothea Lange and the photographer's farm security administration in Americas depressive work period.

The life which comes out from inside this other worldliness worldly imaginary nature. Is from within the humour or amused nature of not having a prerequisite outcome of that nature from within that moment.

Of the, imaginary moment, which makes it as so unpredictable as to introduce a nature of the other worldliness life.

Formed in these ideas of as being humorous and amused. Yet undecidedly as it is a momentary image left to decide on its own outcome as of an appearance.

Photography is like painting, a photographer or a painter transfer's one image by the use of instruments' to another place. Drawing with its' usage imagery, as imaginary moments'.

These instrument also being similar in design fundamentally helps' the photographer or painter at every stage.

Almost or only allowing him preventively not to be creative, these as imagery would be left from the instruments restrictive nature within the boundaries of what they had previously been intended to design.

As from within the imagery attempted by the photographer and painter may not be a truer presentation of what he would ideally of wish to achieve.

Although may be enough to be a notation of what possibilities these instruments might allow the mind to achieve into a realistically interpretation.

Into also the realms of the real world and from out of the other worldliness of the minds imagination or imaginary world as an image of what could be interpreted as the real world.

Until the print process stage or material stage. Tangible process which can be limited in rigid limitations,' they are rigid manipulative processes'.

Rarely creative as these are done within a limitation which are more controlling than under control.

Under the mastership of earlier sciences theology (theory and semiology). Their stringency is such i.e. the daguerreotype, that creativity.

Would not be such a feasible complete idea because creativity is not a destructive process though it is a continual pointer in a truer or more honestly direction towards a more rightly creative nature.

But using the materials' and instruments firstly to a more knowledgeable skilful use would only confirm the ideal/ideology behind these practices' of instrumentation and there use in creativity.

Not, create any further whole concepts even the idea of destroying, destruction of these instruments' including materials' would not leave behind them any purposeful ideal proven throughout the use of these.

And would not rid the possibility of their both as similar ideas' ideology science theory, instrumentation.

Their existence within a theological context, thus far photography also painting instruments'.

Can be seen as both similar in their use to provide a certain kind of future fantasy of reality. Too provide it in a transient transportable form instrumental and textual theory is in a design schematic or optically graphical.

On paper processed these are in material phenomenon, forming a duality, to pointillism in painting or a photograph by whom I would consider a photographer of my admiration.

A landscape filled with these would almost immediately become a reality. Too any observer be it, human or animal would be adaptable to it in all its' configuration's.

An optical instrumental scientific material phenomena would in a sense provide an organic sensibility and attachment actively phenomenological.

In its' own being a sensation of the phenomena would then become as in critical sense an observation not analytical. From an unlimited point of view a so called analysis'.

But used through the concepts' by observation the ideal ideology through observation either philosophical theological, observation for example semiology.

As one cannot analyse knowledge without having knowing it as something other than knowledge itself a form of anything else being possibly known of and about.

Something other cannot obviously exist. Analyses' is not a product of knowing therefore it does not exist as a way of seeing or being knowledge other than that of observational in its' self being.

It thus being only a none existent productive method. Unlike that of observation, I do not analyse a photograph or painting I have observed.

As because I cannot add to it I can only use observational practice's like the instrument and materials' to a more knowledgeable, skilful usage or with the above I could research more knowledge in a theological ideal.

A photographical and painting theological ideal or idealogy, in this I do not see any analyses only of an observational kind of instrumental, material process and practices'.

Impossible to predict unlike advertising the imagery of workers, images of true circumstance's neither decides or undecided by the outcome. But about to be decided, the circumstances', themselves I would only choose to avoid.

The adult humour and amusement is what lies in a dark blind spot between these notions' of decision making.

I would only choose the realities of the photograph to discard the imagery as an unagreable nature of presentation.

From these in the real truer sense of the world as being there in the circumstance. Not wanting the reality of the circumstance to be present. To dictate my eventual decision or indecision upon my destinies as an outcome.

I would look at these pictures' hope as an ideal but would not look at or hold up the circumstance with any amount of hope or as an ideal.

I believe that most people's opinion of photography or art is that of not having any real interest in them other than mere curiosity values of particular's such as the values of personal pleasure or enjoyment.

That they would prefer a subject such as science or financial success in which to have such values' as learning or educational from an experiential point of view a vision of the future.

My personal point of view or a vision of photography and art is that it can be used as a way of learning from and not simply about.

In an educational or experiential point of view also they can both be a vision in which too observationally approach learning.

Educating the individual about there own phenomena as an independent subject or topic. As opposed to the world around them also the world as an independent individual world about them.

In terms of the surrounding being analytically a critical observational point of the presentary moment within their vision of the world around them.

Eye and movement coordination I am told that every pictured image created by this way has been caught taken and photographed including by painting.

The eye is coordinated in the direction of the movement then captured or held in painting. This includes' the position of my eyes' and it as having had movements of coordination.

Of graphic presentation and the image is studied then held by the eye, at a particular height or angled position.

The image or graphical interpretations' of the picture in front of the eye including the size of the graphical image.

An obvious example would be the distance the photograph exists as an ideal In itself image of a idealised view to perfected vision.

Because its' ability to recall ideas even years later unlike a persons memory which is often forgettable as it is selective.

What is really meant by these ideas and imagery is that the people in them, their circumstances' are outlived by the photographic presentation.

Of the ideas and ideals within the imagery the ideal outlives the graphical presentation of the imagery, its' purposes as an image. The photograph outlasts' the peoples' lives and times.

Bibliography

1)   Edward Steichen.

Books on the photographer himself of his experiences as a naval photographer for the navy, Photographic work for the American government, and for Hollywood.

2)   Yousuf karsh.

Books on himself and portraiture.

3)   Lewis Hine.

Books on the poor and poverty in America.

4)   Dorothea Lange.

Head of farm security administration a group of documentary photographer's in America. Books on the poor and poverty in America.

5)   Arthur Felling, (1899-1968).

Weegee, published photographic book's on the cityscape.

6)   Villem Flusser.

Books and articles. Towards an philosophy of photography

7)   Charles Sanders Pierce.

(1839 1914). And his beginning the work on the writing's of semiology.

8)   Hilton Kramer.

Literary critic, and writer on philosophy topical
subjects. Author of a book called,
Understanding philosophy,

9)   Emmanuel Kant (1724-1804).

What is philosophy, a German philosopher, a
note on photographic imagery.

10)   Ansell Adams.

Books about the camera technical; The Negative
and the Print. Also his landscape photographs.

11)   George Seurat.

1859-1891, Painter in pointillism technique in
painting auto biography about his life and work.